NANA'S STORY

from EGYPT to AMERICA

Joyce de Botton

This book which I wrote with lots of love is dedicated to my children, grandchildren and to my future great grandchildren. "The circle of life."

CONTENTS

INTRODUCTION

I WAS BORN "JOCELYNE MAGAR" ON AUGUST 22ND, 1937. While that is still my name appearing on my birth certificate, my passport, and on all of my identification papers, I now go by the name of "Joyce." I never knew why my name changed because in my heart I am still "Jocelyne."

We also called my grandmother "Abuelita." (What do you call the grandmother of your grandmother? Your great great grandmother?) We didn't know that her real name was "Rose" and so why did we call her "Abuelita?" Because her first grandchild "Pepe" was born in Spain. He called her by the Spanish name "Abuelita" which means "Little grandmother." Not one of us grandchildren knew that her name was "Rose" and not "Abuelita."

Why did you my children and grandchildren call my mom "Guine?" Because I had asked my mom what she wanted her first American grandchild, Paul, to call her. Too young at forty years old to be called "Grandmother," she said that Paul should call her by her name "Evelyne." But because Paul could not pronounce the name "Evelyne," he called her instead "Guine." You all adored your Guine.

I grew up on the beaches of Alexandria, Egypt, surrounded by a very large family including my parents, grandparents, brothers, aunts, uncles and many cousins. We were all very close and loving with one another. I had a happy childhood surrounded by many good friends. I met most of them at my French girls school called

"Le Lycée Français" where I graduated with a diploma in Philosophy after finishing high school (Le Baccalaureat). My school friends were: Liliane, Laura, Nicole, Nabila, Daniele, Simone, Fofo (Toy), Joyce L, Touna, Denise, Jacqueline, Dany, Magda, Josette, Viviane, Laila and many more. My best friend Liliane Yeni lived on my street "Rue Prince Ibrahim" in "Camp de Cesar" which was very close to me. So since a young age, I could walk to her house by myself. When I moved to America we got separated and I did not know which part of the world she lived in. We all had left Egypt in a hurry with no goodbyes. We were all of different religions which we knew and respected. Some were Christian, some Muslim, and like myself some were Jewish. We spoke the Mediterranean languages mostly French, Arabic and also we understood many other languages (Greek, Italian etc.) to be able to communicate with each other. At school we played basketball, volleyball and all other gymnastics for girls. Outside the school, we met and played tennis, squash, pingpong and some of us played golf or miniature golf. We all were good swimmers at the pools. I never thought of or even felt our differences. The only time I felt different from some of my classmates was on the Christmas Holidays when my Christian friends got many wonderful presents which were hanging on their beautiful Christmas trees. At that time, I wished I was not Jewish. (We didn't celebrate Hanukkah in Egypt.) No presents for me!

I took ballet classes at the Conservatory. I loved my weekly ballet dancing classes, especially the ballet concerts we gave at the Music Academy. On the big stage we danced in our ballet pointe shoes dressed up in rich sparkling clothes with our faces covered up in adult make up. We looked beautiful and professional.

I was also an Egyptian Girl Scout. With my Egyptian girls scout group, we traveled to the annual European Jamboree representing our country Egypt. The Jamboree was similar to the Olympics. At the start of the event, we walked in a big parade proudly holding up our Egyptian flag. We also sang our Egyptian Anthem which we knew well.

Growing up, I adored my grandmother "Abuelita" (my Mom's Mom) who lived with us in our home sometimes or at her other daughter's house at my favorite aunt "Tante Marcelle's." Abuelita was blond with blue eyes and she had fair skin. She spoke French, Syrian and German. She was educated in a German school. Abuelita told us so many stories about her husband, Elie Anbar who was our late grandfather. He grew up in Damascus, Syria in a mansion which was built by his father Josef Anbar. She told us that we could visit the "Maktab Anbar" in Damascus which became a museum that is open for tourism even today. Also she told us about her own dad (my great grandfather Joseph Aboulafia) who had helped the Rothschilds acquire land in Palestine. In exchange for his help he was rewarded with a street in Israel named after him: "Joseph Aboulafia Street." Years later her grandchildren traveled to Syria and confirmed that all her stories were true. For sure we are the proud descendants of important people.

I also adored my "Grandpapa" and "Grandmaman" who were my dad's parents. They lived in Cairo with the rest of my dad's family. They only spoke Arabic and no French. They were very Egyptian in the way they looked, spoke and wore their clothes. They were wonderful grandparents. They spoiled me by giving me my first camera when I was twelve years old. They taught me to play their favorite game of "TricTrac" (Backgammon) which we enjoyed playing together many times. They took me on vacations to their beautiful summer home in "Ras El Bar." There, away from my strict dad, I was able to sail on the Nile's many "feluccas" with boys and girls together.

I had so much fun!! In Ras El Bar my grandparents gave me my first teenage adventures.

Sadly, I never knew any of their stories. To this day, I do not know where they were born or how they met or what happened to them before settling in Egypt. I had never asked them to tell me their story before I left Egypt. I wish I had asked them.

My Egyptian grandparents "Mr and Mrs Moussa Magar."

My book "Nana's Story from Egypt to America" is dedicated to my grandchildren and to the future generation so they will learn about who I am and where their roots start from. My own parents, whose names are "Salvo and Evelyne Magar" and my two younger brothers' names are "Raymond and Gilbert." This is a story of my journey after leaving Egypt at nineteen years old to settle with my new husband Claude de Botton (Papi) in Philadelphia, USA.

I hope that my story answers some questions about yourself which you could have inherited from me: Why am I addicted to chocolate? or Why do I love taking so many pictures all the time? or Why do I enjoy playing tennis? Or playing a competitive game of cards like "Meshi Meshi" or Bridge with my friends? Why do I love reading a good book to relax? And even, Why do I need to sleep with both feet always out of the covers? You might have inherited my defects too, like being too sensitive or getting angry when someone hurts you, or having a sweet tooth, or being too lazy and avoiding daily exercises, or liking too much traveling around the world with your loved ones. Did you inherit some of my qualities of being positive? Enjoying and appreciating what life offers you, always trying to give love and care for those around you?

I hope that my story will help you learn about your roots from Egypt and the love that is embedded in all of you. You are a part of me and I am a part of you. Forever.

After you read Nana's story, I hope you will be proud of your family history which started in Alexandria, Egypt and continues until today in America. We moved first into seven residences which we could afford then. We finally settled and lived happily for more than fifty years at the home which Papi Claude (who is a builder) had designed and built for us; " Chantilly." Because the color of our new home was white, we called it "Chantilly" which means "Whipped Cream" in English.

PS. I wrote the words "Je Suis Heureuse" in my French daily diaries which I began writing the day I left Egypt in 1956, when I started my life in America. In English it means "I am happy," which I wrote everyday despite my loneliness.

CHAPTER 1

Letter To My Mother Before She Died.

THE MOMENT I RECEIVED THE SAD NEWS THAT MY MOM had a stroke in Brazil, I flew the same day shaking with fear to arrive too late. At the hospital, when the room was completely silent I sat crying next to my mom. She was not moving in the hospital bed. Her eyes were closed. I decided to write her story in a letter, and then read it to her after out loud. I was hoping that deep down in her sick body and mind she could maybe hear me and remember.

MY MAMI'S STORY in a letter:

Her name is Evelyne Magar. Her name was given to her four grand-daughters, Yvette (Eve) de Botton, Nicole Evelyne de Botton, Carina Evelyne Maggar and her youngest took her full name Evelyne Magar. Her name is carried around the world because their parents, her children, live in three different countries. Her daughter Jocelyne de Botton lives in Philadelphia, USA (Me). Raymond Maggar lives in London, England and her son Gilbert Magar lives in Sao Paulo, Brazil.

My mom Evelyne Ambar was born in Alexandria, Egypt. Her dad was killed before she was born. She always used to say to us,"Do not be angry at your dad. I never had one. You are lucky to have one." She is the youngest child of my beautiful grandmother, Rose Ambar (my Abuelita). My Mom had three older sisters, Paula, Henriette, Marcelle and a brother Joseph Ambar. Paula and Joseph lived in the States. Henriette lived in Lebanon and Marcelle in Egypt.

When she was sixteen years old, the mother of my dad (my grandma Magar) asked her dentist if he knew of any blond blue eyed sixteen year old, tall and slim young lady for her son Salvo Magar, who was twenty years old. The dentist gave her the name of my mom. My dad then knocked at her door with the usual fiance box of candies "La Bombonniere." Marcelle opened the door. He kissed her and told her she was very pretty. She said, "I am not your fiance, my sister Evelyne is but she is locked in the bathroom and my mom is screaming for her to get out for you."

They got married because their parents told them to marry even though they both did not want to marry. My dad loved the wrong girl-friend and my mom was too young and innocent.

Their first son, Elis, was born and two years later, Jocelyne (me) was born. My brother was very special to me. He protected me, played with me and everyone who saw us together admired the bond we had. We adored each other. But at the age of seven, Elis died suddenly. My mom could not recover. Her dad and her first born had died too early. I missed that brother who was my partner and my protector. He was gone and did not return. The school picture arrived home after his death. I stole it to put it under my pillow. I kissed my brother's picture every night for almost a year until my second brother Raymond was born. Five years later her second son Gilbert was born.

Her three children lived in three different countries. But my mom always managed to keep us united and always loving and supporting each other, including loving each other's family even though we lived oceans apart. She taught us how to love our children and more impor-tantly to make sure they respected, protected and loved each other. But she never stopped missing her first born Elis. She said, "Death is not the end; Forgetting is the end."

I met my husband Claude de Botton on a beach at night, attracted to the direction where he was sitting alone on the sand watching the stars. Destiny brought us together that night. He had just arrived tired from Philadelphia where he was studying Civil Engineering at the University of Pennsylvania in Philadelphia. He had lived in Switzerland away from home since the age of thirteen where he was educated in a boarding school called "Le Rosey." Right after that, he went to continue his studies in Philadelphia. I had not met him in Egypt before, even though his parents lived not far from us in Alexandria. It was love at first sight. My big surprise was going to his house and finding the same school picture of my dead brother in his drawer. I screamed because Claude was sitting on the same row as Elis, in the same class picture. So I realized that I did kiss my husband's picture for a whole year a long time before.

My mom then found out that Claude was born on the same date, same hospital, same doctor who delivered her son. We married in an emergency under the bombs of the Suez Canal War (the war between Egypt and Israel). So strange that our wedding date is the exact same date of her son's death. She got back her son with my husband on December 12th, 1956.

Because of this war, she had to run away from her birth land with her husband (my father) and her sons, leaving everything behind. They could not go anywhere because they were Egyptian refugees accepted only in very few places. They settled in Brazil where they arrived with no money (the Egyptians took it all) and they did not speak the Portuguese language.

As for me, in the middle of the night I left Egypt on the first plane, running away with my husband Claude who had a student visa to be able to live in the States. We did not have money and I did not speak English, just like her. Her first grandson, Paul de Botton, was born far away and she saw him for the first time when he was three years old. As for her son, Raymond, he was transferred to London at the age of twenty-one. Later, he became the CEO of American Express in London. His daughter, Carina Evelyne, was born in London. Her other son, Gilbert, gave his daughter her full name "Evelyne Magar." She was born in Brazil.

My mom spoke four languages fluently: French, Arabic, Portuguese and some English. She watched the news in four different languages on four different channels. She could discuss an event from different angles. My mom read a book in one day no matter if it was written in French, English or Portuguese. My mom was a Bridge champion among much younger players. My mom taught me her advice in French, which I will try to translate in English.

"Your face may have wrinkles but your heart never gets any."

(Ton visage peut avoir des rides mais ton coeur ne les a jamais.)

"Your life is a garden. You plant nothing and you get nothing. If you plant seeds of love and friendship, you will find your garden blooming with flowers of all colors."

(Ta vie est un jardin. Tu ne plantes rien, tu n'as rien. Mais si tu plantes amour et amitiés, ton jardin sera fleuri avec toutes les couleurs des fleurs.)

"If nobody calls you, and you think you are forgotten, pick up the phone and you call everyone."

(Si personne ne te téléphone et que tu te crois oubliée prends toi le téléphone et appelles tout le monde.)

"When you don't like the way you look in a mirror, just know they don't know how to make good quality mirrors anymore."

(Si tu t'embêtes a te regarder au miroir c'est la faute du miroir qui est de mauvaise qualité, pas comme le passé.)

"If you do not like yourself in a picture, hide it, but look at it again a few years later. For sure you will love the way you used to look in the past."

(Si tu n'aimes pas ta photo, caches la et vois la des années plus tard. Et alors tu aimeras beaucoup cette photo du passe.)

"Appreciate what you have. Do not cry for what you do not have, then your tears will wash away what you have."

(Apprécies ce que tu as. Ne pleures pas pour ce que tu n'as pas car alors tes larmes vont effacer ce que tu as.)

"Give joy around you and you will become the happy one."

(Donnes de la joie autour de toi et tu seras la plus heureuse.)

"Show me your friends and I will tell you who you are."

(Montres moi tes amis et je te dirai qui tu es.)

"Give with a warm hand and not with a cold hand. (It will be cold when you die.)"

(Donnes avec une main chaude et pas avec une main froide.)

"Do not wait for tomorrow what you can do today."

(Ne remets jamais a demain ce que tu peux faire aujourd'hui.)

"Do not only exercise sports for your body. Play games of cards to exercise sports for the mind which is very important too."

(Ne fais pas seulement des exercices pour le corps car il faut aussi faire des exercises pour la tête en jouant les cartes. C'est aussi important.)

My mom played cards almost every day until she died at ninety-five after winning a tournament of Bridge. I shall follow her wisdom and I will continue her lessons with my own family through generations. Thank you mami. You have enriched each one of us with your love and your teaching of love.

Looking at my mother laying in the hospital bed in a coma with her eyes closed, I continued reading to her my letter:

"Mami, right now I am crying next to you because I see you suffer too much and your mind is still very sharp. Mami it hurts too much. We are all around you… your children, your grandchildren. They all flew from far away to spend time with you. They adore you even if they were raised far from you. I know that someday, maybe soon, I shall lose you and you will then join your dad, your mom, your son, your husband, your sisters and your brother. Your image is reflected in each one of us, who are lucky to get a piece of you. We shall try to follow your teachings of happiness, generous love, positive attitude at all times, pride in yourself, forgiving and never complaining.

I kissed her hand, the good one which was not paralyzed. I told her that I shall miss this hand that I held on to when I was a little girl so I couldn't fall down. This hand which caressed me when I was sick or crying. I was kissing the strong hand which had loved and guided me through all my life. She died right after.

CHAPTER 2

World War II When German Bombs Fell Over Egypt.

I WAS FIVE YEARS OLD WHEN IN 1942, IN THE MIDDLE OF World War II, Hitler's armies approached Egypt. They fought first the battle of "Tobruk" then a few months later they fought (much closer to us) the battle of El Alamein which marked the end of World War II in North Africa. The British armies (led by commander Montgomery) fought the German armies (led by general Rommel). They dropped many bombs on top of us in Alexandria. There were first loud sirens in the middle of the night, a signal for us to leave our beds fast and run in our pajamas to hide underground. All of us in the building had to go down the stairs in a hurry, carrying the young ones crying in their mother's arms. The German bombs were very scary, exploding dangerously over us. I thought I was going to die so young at five years old and my parents thought that as soon as the Germans would win again, they would round us up and take all of us to German camps.

Instead, the British and their allies won the Al Amein battle in Egypt in October 1942, defeating Hitler's German armies.

What a relief for us!! If the Germans had won in Egypt, we would have been on our way to Auschwitz!!! World War II had arrived too close to us.

In the meantime, I almost died that night because the building I was sleeping in (at a friend's place away from my family) was hit by the bombs. I was screaming the whole night calling for my mother. Until now I scream when I hear any loud noises, especially the July 4th fireworks. My parents said that it was a miracle that I had survived.

Another nightmare happened to me when I was four years old. My brother Elis and I were two and a half years apart. We were inseparable.

One night, my parents had gone out to a friend's party and left us with a babysitter. "Jossy, come fast" Elis screamed from the bathroom, "and look at my pipi. It's all blood." We did not know how to reach my parents, and the babysitter did not know how to use a phone. I called my uncle David, a doctor whose phone number I knew by heart. He told me that he was sending an ambulance immediately and that the babysitter should prepare my brother for the hospital.

We tried to reach my parents but ultimately we failed. Most households did not have a telephone. I looked at my scared brother, an image I can still remember in my mind. I saw him leave home on a stretcher being carried down to the ambulance. There was fear and pain in his eyes. He was screaming "Mami Mami." That was the last time I saw my brother. He died at the hospital before my parents returned.

Even though it was the last time I saw him, I still remember playing "Cache Cache" or ""Hide-and-seek" with my brother the same night he got sick and he was taken away. I adored my older brother Elis. He adored me. He was my best friend at the start of my life.

My mother was heartbroken after his death. She would cry for hours each day. I barely saw my mother not crying during the next few months. She was always dressed in black. When she looked at me, she cried even more. This broke my heart. In my little mind I thought that she resented me and wished it was me dead instead of my brother because Elis was the golden child. He was handsome and smart. Our quiet house was a constant reminder of the loved one that we had lost. I spent most nights crying. I cried for my brother, for my parents, and for myself.

The International Tennis Championships in Alexandria.

From 1925 on, the International Tennis Championships were held every year in Alexandria and later in Cairo. Those tournaments were played at the "Sporting Club" tennis courts where I used to play tennis myself. All the famous tennis players came from all different countries in the world to compete in Alexandria. It was the most important event of the year. One time, the American tennis player named Mel Fox fell in love with me. I was sixteen years old. It was at the Tennis Farewell Ball at the club. He sang to me on the microphone the song "I Am a Stranger in Paradise" in front of the whole audience. Then he asked my parents to marry me and take me with him to America where he promised that I would have a wonderful life. My mom answered him politely that her daughter could not survive leaving her family behind and going to America, no matter how wonderful life is there. "She will marry a boy from Egypt, and they will live happily in their own country among their families and friends. So sorry young man!!" She never told me about this conversation with the American player.

Yes, I did marry in Egypt the boy next door (Papi), but he did take me to live in America.

I guess that my destiny was prewritten for me to live in America.

CHAPTER 3

How We Met.

My parents were very strict. Until seventeen I was ordered to do my school work, babysit my brothers and be home before dark. We belonged to a country club where I played tennis and swam in the pool with my friends. But going to parties was forbidden and absolutely no boys were allowed to even call me on the house phone. I would spend most nights with my brothers at home studying. We were fortunate to have our neighbors who were the same age as the three of us; the Cohens, the Rousseaus and the Zayans. We would meet every day after school and we had so much fun together. My friends were free to date and go to parties and I couldn't do the same. My best friend at that time was my cousin, Rolande. Since we were young, we were attached by the hip. When I got all of my work done, I would take a bus by myself to spend the night at her house. It was the freedom I looked for.

The summer of 1955 I was invited to go to my close friend Lucie Pichotto's seventeenth birthday party which was being held at her summer home on the beach of Agami. Not feeling optimistic, but dying to go to her party I begged my parents for several days to allow me to go. Each conversation ended in a stern "No way! Too far! Who will drive you all the way to the beach?" I would spend nights imagining what fun the party would be and what I would be missing. The night of the party, I was feeling sad and depressed.

I decided to spend the night at my cousin's house. I kept my school uniform on and my flat ugly shoes thinking we would hang out and go to sleep. But when I arrived at her home, Rolande told me she was getting ready to go to Lucie's birthday party with her older brother Lorys, who would be driving her to Agami. A feeling of excitement washed over me. This was my time to escape my parents' rules and have fun. My parents thought I was spending the night at Rolande's house so they would never find out that I went to the party. I borrowed Rolande's party clothes but kept my ugly flat shoes. When we arrived at Lucie's birthday party we found lots of well dressed guests, beautiful girls in high heels, drinking, smoking and dancing to American music. Not having been allowed to attend parties, I was insecure. I felt ugly, shy and inexperienced compared to the other girls. I felt like a villager in a town; an outsider. My insecurities were magnified through my guilt for lying to my parents. Feeling sad and guilty, I walked towards Rolande to tell her I wanted to leave.

That is when I saw him, a gorgeous boy dressed in all white. His black curly hair perfectly contrasted with his white and elegant outfit. He was standing talking quietly to a friend. He seemed mature and disinterested in drinking and partying. He was walking away from the noise and making his way to the beach, where he found a place to sit on the sand close to the sea. I approached him slowly, building my courage to speak to him. I stopped from behind him and quietly said, "Do you want some company?" He looked at me surprised and responded, "Sure, please sit next to me." We exchanged names, me "Joyce Magar " and him "Claude de Botton." While he did not speak much about himself, I learned he had arrived from America that same night where he had been attending a university in America. He told me he was very tired but his best friend Freddy, dragged him to the party against his will. Our connection was instant and conversation was easy and comfortable. He asked me about myself and taught me the names of the stars shining above us. He was focused on me and I was smitten by this handsome man sitting close to me. I remembered that my mother's best friend, Aunt Renee (his mother's sister) had a nephew who was studying in America. So it was Claude who was Aunt Renee's nephew. We spoke for a long time in the dark of the night. We had never crossed paths as he spent much time away from home since he was twelve years old. As time passed too fast, we heard Rolande's voice from far calling my name. She was ready to go. Unsure of how we would reconnect Claude said, "Give me your telephone number before you leave." I responded "No way, no boys are allowed to call me on the phone or I will be punished." While I was running back to the party, I heard him scream to me "Goodbye Cinderella."

I spent the night dreaming of the boy that I met in Agami Beach. He called me the next day when I returned home. I was surprised but so happy to hear his voice and my heart started beating fast. "Will you go to the movies with me?" I was shocked. Claude had found me and rang my telephone. "How did you find me?" I asked. He replied, "I asked my Aunt Reneé because you told me last night that she was your mother's best friend." Unable to make the decision whether to go out with him alone without my father's consent I told him, "You have to ask for my father's permission." That same day Claude showed up at my doorstep and asked my dad his permission to take me to the movies. Surprisingly, my father did not slam the door in his face. Instead, in a stern voice my father told him, "Young man, do you have any serious intentions for my daughter before you take her out to the movies?" The intention my father was referring to was marrying me. He continued, "If you do, then you can take her out." I was elated and surprised by my father's permission. Later, Claude told me that he said 'yes' to dad because in his mind the intentions he really promised him were to have fun with a summer girlfriend before he goes back to America to the university. It was not the promise to marry me at all. So we happily went out to the movies. That day happened to be the first date in my life. I was seventeen, just a month away from my eighteenth birthday.

CHAPTER 4

Summer of 1955 Dating Claude.

After Claude had agreed that he had "intentions" my Dad gave us permission to date. He knew that this young man came from a rich, Jewish prominent family that he knew well in Alexandria; the "de Botton family." Suddenly at seventeen Claude and I spent the best summer in 1955. We went sailing, dancing, dining at chic restaurants and seeing the best shows in town. He certainly made me feel like "Cinderella" from the moment we met. I had a super social life and I turned from a young girl to an adult because my frog had turned into a prince. Claude took me to many parties of our new friends who were Christians, Muslims, Jews, Arabs, Italians, French, Greeks and all fun people. We had developed a wonderful close friendship among all of them. What I remember most is that it did not matter what color the skin or where they came from: We were all Egyptian friends.

We went to bathe and play "racquets" and surf at our favorite beach "Sidi Bishr." We went sailing at the "Club Nautique" on the port of the Blue Mediterranean sea and stopped to bathe at "Ramlah Beyda" (White Sands). We joined friends at the Sporting Club playing tennis, golf, swimming in the pools and eating delicious desserts "babas," meringues, eclairs au chocolat and the best ice creams in town. My parents also played card games daily with Claude's parents at our country club. But the best was when Claude picked me up at night in his dad's big blue car (a Nash) to go dancing at "The Romance" the popular and chic dancing place or "Montaza Palace" in the ex king Farouk palace with a live band. Claude used all his Bar Mitzvah gold to make me a gold key chain with letters C & J our initials tied forever.

Dating in Egypt was almost impossible. If you were not married and were caught holding hands or kissing you were automatically taken to jail. At every corner stood "Police des Moeurs." Also my Mom had warned me that in Alexandria everyone knew everyone and that my "reputation" was the most important thing for a girl. She advised me to be careful and not do anything I might regret. Claude had to leave at the end of August to go back to Philadelphia, so we desperately needed to be left alone. Sometimes we chose the cemetery where no one could bother us. It was definitely not the most romantic place surrounded by only ghosts.

Having not seen him around in Egypt, he told me that since he was thirteen years old that he lived first in an all boys boarding school in Switzerland called "Le Rosey," and later studied in America at the University of Pennsylvania in Philadelphia. That is why I had not seen him much. He grew up away from his family in Egypt.

He was my first love and I was also his first love. We had a short time dating, less than two months since we met. We were separated for ten months until June of 1956 with no possible contact except for letters. Phone calls were not only very expensive but it was hard to hear each other on terrible lines. Everyday I wrote him a long and detailed letter which he saved and later made into an album titled "Lettres de Joyce 1955-1956" in gold letters. (350 letters I sent!)

CHAPTER 5

The Suez Canal War That Changed My Life.

IN 1956, THE SUEZ CANAL WAR BROKE OUT. IT CHANGED my life, the lives of my family members and the lives of many Jews whose families had lived in Egypt for hundreds of years.

The Suez Canal War was a product of a fight for power and dominance over the very important Suez Canal. Gamal Abdel Nasser, the president of Egypt at the time, wanted control over the Western world. To obtain power, he nationalized the Suez Canal preventing foreign transports across the Middle East. This decision ignited fury amongst the Israeli, British and French governments. The three countries joined armed forces and bombarded Egypt, mostly the port of Alexandria. We Egyptian Jews were so scared because those Israeli bombs kept exploding on top of our homes. Could you imagine if Israel bombed America? How would you feel?

President Nasser was infuriated. He ordered all Jews to leave Egypt as soon as possible. Terrified, they left in a hurry while the Egyptians overtook their homes, their businesses, their belongings and their bank accounts. They would be arrested if they found anyone carrying more than 200 livres ($100) and no personal jewelry or valuables were allowed to be taken out. What was most painful for us citizens was that our Egyptian passports were revoked and we became stateless to the world.

One night in particular remains vivid in my mind. While my family and I were sleeping, we were awakened by those loud noises that I recognised and feared. I heard the elevator stop followed by powerful stomps and forceful voices. My neighbors were seized from their apartments on the third floor and were immediately taken to prison camps. They were innocent of any kind of crimes.

Fearful for our lives, the intimidating tactics employed by Nasser reminded us that not so long ago the Jews were arrested and murdered in Germany. We had seen the torment and violence inflicted upon them and knew our only option for safety was to follow Nasser's orders. We did not want to repeat history and wait. We left in a hurry leaving behind all that we had ever known.

CHAPTER 6

Claude Comes Back Home From America.

CLAUDE CAME BACK HOME IN JUNE OF 1956. AFTER SO many letters exchanged between us, we knew each other better than anyone else. Our love had been tested through our long separation.

But our happy romance did not last long. The Suez Canal war had broken out.

Suddenly, all of our Egyptian entourage stopped being friendly. They were afraid of being seen close to us. They wanted us to leave because we were becoming a problem in their lives.

Every year at Passover Seder my family used to thank God for our exit out of Egypt! I just could not understand. Why were we praying around the table with our prayer books while still in Egypt, having never left Egypt? Why did we have to thank God? We were the chosen people having to get out again. Friends and family prepared to leave wherever refugees were accepted. My dad's sister's family,the Haim family went to Israel. My mom's family and her sister Marcelle's family went to join their sister Henriette Haiat in Brazil. As for Claude's family, they settled in Europe mostly in London. Because of Claude's student visa, we could live in America while no one else was allowed entry.

CHAPTER 7

Testing Our Love.

ONE MORNING, PAPI CALLED TO TELL ME HIS FATHER wanted to speak with me and that a chauffeur would be waiting in the driveway. Without knowledge of what this meeting would be about I quickly changed, telling no one of my whereabouts. I trembled with fear. I had never spoken with his father alone, only in Claude's presence.

I had rarely seen him smile as he was a private and serious man. He was powerful and intimidating. He commanded respect from everyone surrounding him. He fathered his sons much like one would expect from a man with his reputation. They were obedient, respectful and would not dare to step away from the path that he had set for them. After his Bar Mitzvah, Claude studied in Switzerland in keeping with his father's orders. There he excelled in all sports and won many awards including hockey, swimming and tennis. At the age of sixteen and following his time in Switzerland, Papi would begin his studies at the University of Pennsylvania in Philadelphia. It was here that he would get his Bachelor diploma in Civil Engineering.

Why was I summoned by Claude's father? What would he ask me? Did he believe my love for his son or did he resent me because he thought I wanted their money? Was he going to write me a check so I would leave Claude to go back by himself to America? I had heard the stories of forbidden love and feared our love would be punished and that we would have to separate. I arrived at his father's office lacking confidence. He was seated at his desk with a sternness on his face. His jaw tightened and his posture was stiff, much like a teacher. As I stood there, I hid my nervousness with a smile. His intensity made me shy.

After what seemed like hours had gone by his deep voice commanded my attention. "Claude told me he wants to bring you to America when he goes back to the University." My heart fluttered at the thought of a future for us. "This is what I need to know" he said, "do you love my son? Are you willing to risk everything to be with him?" I nodded my head, failing to meet his eyes. "We are in the midst of a war that will change everything you have ever known," he continued, "he will lose everything, you will be poor and alone, far away from your family. As you only speak French and Arabic, you will have to learn English with no one to help you. You are nineteen years old and he is twenty-one years old. You are both very young." His voice began to rise, "Are you sure you love him?" His intimidation did not scare me. The unknown of our future frightened me, but despite all of this, my love for Claude was indefinite. I had seemed to gain my confidence back "I do love him, no matter how poor we shall be but we will survive together. I will follow him anywhere." His father thanked me and left because he got the answer he needed. I was willing and ready to leave Egypt and go to America despite his speech to make me aware of my difficult and hard future ahead.

The irony of this meeting is that my in-laws (Dada and Meme) loved visiting us in America as often as they could. I used to take good care of them and attended to all their needs as the best daughter-in-law one could ever have. Claude did not miss a day at the office and left us to make plans for the day without him. They loved staying in America. They enjoyed spending time with all our American friends who spoiled them with their friendships. That is why they kept coming back, especially on the Christmas holidays when they visited us from the beginning of December to the end of February.

I loved Claude. He loved me. While I was devastated to leave my loved ones behind in Egypt I had no choice. It was the safest option. Soon after, we would all be forced out of Egypt anyway. My parents settled in Brazil and Claude's parents settled in England. Our family had been separated. Claude and I were the only ones with the opportunity to go to the United States. It was only the two of us who could live in America because of his student visa.

CHAPTER 8

My Engagement and Wedding in Egypt.

CLAUDE CALLED ME TO SAY THAT HIS DAD'S FRIEND, Monsieur Vatouri, had spoken with my dad to discuss the amount of my dowry which was very important for girls to marry at that time. It was the same as a price tag on the bride-to-be. She was worth much more if her dowry was high. Claude had been waiting behind closed doors for a long time, scared that the arrangement with my dad could not be made and that he could not marry me. It all depended on how much dowry my dad could afford. Claude did not care how much I was worth. As soon as Mr. Vatouri came out and told him that the deal was made, he called me to let me know that we were engaged! The next call from Claude was, "I got news from my parents. We are getting married next week on Wednesday as soon as possible because of the ongoing war. It will be a simple wedding at my home with only close family."

Afraid to draw the furious Arab attention, Claude's dad ordered me to not wear a bridal dress but rather a simple suit at my wedding. I refused his order and went to their home in a suit, but immediately changed my clothes at their neighbor's house and came out from the elevator dressed in white. My mom had sewn a beautiful bridal gown for me in the middle of the night. While waiting for me in a corner of the room, Claude was wearing his cousin's wedding suit which was a couple sizes bigger than him. He didn't have time to buy a new suit. My wedding day would ironically be one of the saddest days of my life. We knew that the next day we would have to leave Egypt, wondering if we would ever see each other again.

Everyone was wearing black, everyone was crying because no one knew what would happen after the wedding. Would we meet again somewhere? Why were we all punished because we were born Jewish in our country Egypt? I always dreamt of a big wedding. This was far from it.

A rabbi arrived through the back door to bless the ceremony. I could not stop crying under my white veil. As he pronounced us man and wife, I looked around the room and wondered if I would ever see the faces of my loved ones again.

My grandfather was a proud Egyptian wearing his "Tarbouche" hat the Egyptian red hat. He preferred to die rather than leave his beloved country. Why were we punished this way in our Alexandria, our birth land? All my friends had already left Egypt. I was suddenly stripped of my identity and my citizenship. My country did not want me anymore. I should leave as soon as possible and I could not carry with me anything that I owned. I heard that many people, on the night before their departures, swallowed their wedding ring's diamond stone that they had wrapped in chewing gum to protect it and to help the swallowing as easily as big pills. They recovered the diamond later, picking it up from inside the toilet. That is the way they passed the Egyptian Customs. Their wedding ring was one thing they would not separate from.

I was a refugee, running away and leaving my world behind. We left everything behind us, home, family, friends in a rush. Was being Jewish a crime? The importance at this time was that we were married and my name had changed on my passport (Italian as my husband's) from Jocelyne Magar to Jocelyne de Botton born 8/22/1937 in Egypt. We were flying to America where Claude was registered at the University of Pennsylvania and our status was "students." The key for entering the USA.

CHAPTER 9

Wedding Night in Egypt.

AFTER THE CEREMONY WHICH WAS FAST AND SIMPLE, we had a room reserved in a luxury hotel in Alexandria for our wedding night. In our little prepared suitcase was my satin embroidered nightgown set from my bride's "Trousseau" (bridal clothes prepared in a short time by my Mom). Claude had his satin new pajama set too. But under those new and luxurious clothes for us to wear were two scared and unprepared virgins.

My Mom kept telling me that I shall be hurt and bleeding. Her advice was "Drink lots of champagne and then you will not have too much pain." As for Claude's mother, she put in his suitcase without any explanation a big jar of vaseline to "protect ourselves." We did not know what we were supposed to do with this vaseline. There were no computers, Ipads or cell phones to teach us love and sex which kept us very ignorant. We had been taught that sex was "dirty" all our lives. Remembering my mother's advice, I asked my new husband to first order me a bottle of champagne. I had never touched alcohol before so I got drunk fast and went to sleep fast. The next morning I awoke and told Claude that I was relieved and happy that I had no pain from the sex. He answered, "We did not have sex my love because you were fast asleep!!" So I left Egypt, a married lady and a virgin!!!

CHAPTER 10

Leaving Egypt.

MY HUSBAND TOLD ME TO BE READY TO LEAVE Alexandria and go by train to Cairo. There we would catch a plane which would fly to Switzerland first, then to Paris then to America. It was great news for me that we would stop in Paris. Here we would drop his young brother Alain, who was flying with us to live at his Uncle Maurice de Botton's home. In Paris, we would spend a night with his French family and then fly to Philadelphia. This would be our honeymoon. One night in Paris.

We boarded a train from Alexandria to Cairo. For the first time with my husband after our wedding, I was dreaming of a romantic ride where I would be hugged and kissed. Instead, he gave me a hat box to put on my lap through the whole ride to Cairo. The whole time he was much more interested in that hat box than me!! He told me that it was his Mom's makeup (but she was not coming with us!!) I was surprised and could not understand the reason I was to hold this box tightly through the whole train ride. As a shy, new wife I didn't ask questions and did what he ordered me to do.

Little did I know that this box I was holding on my lap among a train full of hateful Arabs (who were looking at this blond foreigner) contained his family jewelry. It was the most dangerous act that I was completely unaware of.

In the box I was carrying on my lap were hidden jewels. If they had been discovered by the Arabs we would have been arrested and sent to jail, unable to leave Egypt.

Nobody asked my permission or told me that the box on my lap was not my mother in law's makeup. All I was thinking as a new romantic bride was "Please kiss me Claude and love me instead of this stupid box I am carrying!" But all he kept whispering in my ears throughout the whole train ride was, "Take well care, watch it well, keep an eye over the box. Do not drop it. This is my mother's makeup!" Such a big lie from my new husband!

If I knew the truth, I would have been shaking with fear with all those Arab eyes looking at me the blond foreigner they all hated. At the Cairo airport we sat down to eat lunch with a man I didn't know. Suddenly I panicked and told Claude that his mother's makeup had disappeared. He comforted me and told me that the box filled with personal jewels was on its way to be saved and kept in Switzerland.

No one thanked me for my courageous and very dangerous act. For them it was a mission accomplished!

CHAPTER 11

Arriving in America.

FROM PARIS WHERE WE HAD SPENT OUR FIRST NIGHT AS husband and wife, we flew to Philadelphia. But I was very sick on the plane so the pilot contacted Philadelphia to send us an ambulance at the Philadelphia airport. As soon as the plane landed, I was driven to the University of Pennsylvania Hospital. Claude left me in a ward with five other beds. He rushed out because he had to register immediately for his classes at the University of Pennsylvania.

Alone, not speaking English, no one understood my french or my Arabic language. I was confused. I had a high fever and started to hallucinate. Because the nurse was African American, I thought she was an Egyptian nurse who only spoke Arabic. I screamed to her in Arabic for her to get my husband. At one point, she read my thermometer and she exclaimed to another nurse, "It's a very high fever at 104." I thought I was dead because the thermometers at home don't go higher than 41!

They put me to sleep by drugging this crazy woman talking some foreign language which no one could understand. I was scared. I was very sick while resting in my corner bed among four other beds. Everyday at three o'clock the doors opened up for all the patients' visitors who came with flowers and sat talking to the other women in the room. No one came for me so I hid under the sheets and cried silently. I dreamt of my family who would come to visit me too. One day when the visitors arrived, I heard my name called "Jocelyne de Botton." I was surprised because I didn't know anyone in America. It was Faye, my first American friend, who until now is one of my best friends. I was not invisible anymore. I asked her how she found me? She told me that Claude had asked his friend Herby at Penn if his girlfriend could speak French because his wife didn't speak English and was alone in the University Hospital next door. She made me so happy to have a visitor of my own for the first time.

my Picture in Egypt

my Parents & brothers

in America

my mom & 2 brothers

in Egypt

My Parents wedding

at Temple dreaming of my wedding

my class at the Lycée Français

Our home "Chantilly"

our 6th wife on grandchild in

my grandma

Abuelita

Last time at a wedding

dreaming of my next wedding

my handsome Claude in front of the Pyramids

Claude & me leaving Egypt

in front of the Pyramids

Raymond & Gérard

my 2 younger brothers

Henri & Dodo, Claude's Parents

Welcoming us in Egypt

Mr. Sadat receive my family

3 generations: Me, Mami, Abuelita

I missed Egypt, my Paradise lost

At the Sadat home in the study of the late Egyptian president from left are Yvette de Botton, Paul de Botton, Joyce de Botton, Jihan Sadat, Claude de Botton and Moise de Botton.

JOYCE de BOTTON
'... I still miss it all'

Dr Richard Rothman (Rothman Institute) was a Super achiever

From left are Dr. Richard H. Rothman, Joyce de Botton and Walter H. Annenberg

38

I announce as chairman of SDF
the names of the Super Achievers -

May 6 —
the day
for annual
"Salute" Gala

Saturday, May 6 is the banner day,
and the Franklin Institute the locale,
of the 1978 "Salute to Super Achievers." Chairman Joyce de Botton has
also announced that selection of eight
recipients of the coveted award has
been completed.

Yvette
surprises me
singing to me
at my charity
"La Grande
fête"
"You don't give
me any flowers"

I chairman of Tay Sacks ball which
I called it in french "La Grande fête"

Our family Vacations

Claude Isidore de Botton Family

LEST WE FORGET

The Delaware County Veteran Memorial

The "Hall of prayers" the POWS To return and sit on the empty chair waiting for them.

Grandma Meme, Papi, Nana, Grandma Guine (Standing)
Will, Alessandra, Misha, Ariela, Alycia, Claudia, Brooke (Seated)
(This picture was taken before Michael, Jack and Dani were
born in America.)

Grandma Meme, Yvette, Papi, Nana, Paul, Grandma Guine,
and Nicole.

CHAPTER 12

Starting Life in America.

I WAS VERY COLD WHEN I ARRIVED IN JANUARY OF 1957 in America. In Egypt, I had never seen the snow. We were also very poor. We first lived in a basement of a small apartment in Germantown, PA. Then we lived in an alcoholic old woman's home attic in Bala Cynwyd. She hated us when she found out that we were Jewish. She forbade us to sit in her living room or the den. During the days when Claude was away at school, she would beat me. Claude went to school, leaving at 7 am and returning at 11 pm. I was pregnant at the time with my son Paul. Due to my pregnancy, I became very sick with nausea, weakness and often fainted. Because of my bad condition, Claude felt it would be wiser to have me boarding somewhere in someone's house so I would not be alone. I had already gone to the hospital many times to receive the IVs I needed.

In Egypt I called Claude by his English nickname which I lovingly gave to him "Pussy" (cat). He was my Pussy. I loved my Pussy. When he went to America, I wrote to him every day a long letter written in French and starting with "My Pussy." Well... when I came to America I sure didn't know what the word Pussy meant in the English language. I got into trouble many times bringing lots of laughter and lots of jokes at my expense to my new American friends. So I changed his nickname to "Mon Cheri" which means 'My Love'in French. Much better.

I loved playing the card game called Bridge. One day I went to play in a Bridge tournament in town with my girlfriend Sue

43

Sternberg. She was my Bridge partner that day. The couple we played against was Omar Sharif, the famous Egyptian movie star and his Bridge partner. Omar Sharif asked me, "Where do you come from?" I answered him,"Where you come from!" He was annoyed and asked me again. Again I answered him, "Where you come from!" He said, "I asked you first. Where do you come from?" So I started speaking in Arabic. Taken by surprise by this blonde American woman speaking in his own language, he invited us to join him at the bar for a drink after the tournament. When the game was over, Sue was furious at me. I had refused to go and meet the handsome, big celebrity movie star at the bar and chose to go home instead. I told her that my own Omar Sharif was waiting for me at home. She never forgave me for missing this unbelievable opportunity.

I remember other situations which happened to me because of my poor English language. Claude needed to have his shirts ironed because I had burnt the last ones. I found out that there was a cleaner called "Arcadia" not far from the only two places I knew to walk to. One was the Bala Cynwyd post office, where I used to mail my letters to my family in Brazil and the other place was the Bala Cynwyd train station where I dropped Claude for his train rides in the mornings and picked him up in the evenings on his returns. That day I packed up two of his shirts in a plastic bag along with some money in case I had to pay. When I arrived at Arcadia, I asked someone there if he could iron my husband's skirts. Laughing he said, "Is your husband born in Scotland and does he wear skirts? I answered, "No, my husband was born in Egypt." He explained to me that they never iron Arab skirts!! I looked at all those shirts hanging on top of the store and told him, "Yes you do. Look at all those above there that are already ironed." Annoyed and in a teacher's voice he replied, "Lady, those are not men's skirts they are men's shirts!!" I felt ashamed of myself and could cry of my stupidity in America.

One day, I accidentally walked over the old lady's tomato plants. She was so angry at me that she started beating me. When Claude called me to ask how I was doing, I told him what was going on. Since he did not own a car, he asked his friend Paul Sude to drive him back to me. When he arrived, we quickly packed and drove away before this horrible woman came back from shopping.

All we could afford after boarding in the lady's attic was a cheap room in a hotel on Walnut Street (52nd) which we soon learned also rented to the local prostitutes by the hour. So the only friends I made there were prostitutes who robbed me of the few things I still owned. Longing for friendship, I lent them money and suitcases which were never returned.

When I thought I might be pregnant, I asked Claude what I should do?? He did not know either. He wished that I was not pregnant because he feared that he could not feed us with no money. He found a doctor who took my urine and told us that if the rabbit dies, he will call to tell us that I was pregnant. Claude was worried and when the doctor called us the next day to tell us that the rabbit had died, he almost fainted.

Months later, my water broke. Claude was about to leave me alone in our Brierhurst Hotel room because he needed to fly to Canada to find work. It was lucky that my water broke just as he was about to fly away. In his excitement, he called the police instead of the ambulance. The police car drove us to the Pennsylvania Hospital. Because I was in labor, Paul was almost born in a police car. As his baby head was on its way out, Claude kept closing my legs together to stop him from being born.

My First Child Paul Was Born January 13th, 1958 in America.

At the University Hospital of Pennsylvania, everyday at 4pm, all the mothers gathered with their visitors at the nursery window to proudly show them their new born baby. A nurse would walk right up to the window holding one baby at a time and present it to the family. I felt so alone. I had no visitor to see my baby Paul. Miserable, I cried thinking of my family who was not present during this incredible and emotional moment for me. To hurt me even more, there was a large American family standing close to me looking at the baby on the nurse' s arm from the other side of the window. I heard them discussing how beautiful their baby was and how cute he was!! "He has his daddy's chin, and his mother's round face. Look at his head full of black hair!!! He does look like his grandfather! He is the most adorable baby boy we have ever seen!!!"

They were all loud and very happy, talking at the same time until the nurse made them a sign by pointing at the baby and explaining to them that this baby whom she was showing now was NOT their baby.... but mine!!!!!

Suddenly I forgot that I was alone. I proudly admired the beautiful little baby boy held on the nurse's arm. My heart was full of love because he was definitely my own American son and no one else's.

My Second Child Yvette was Born July 30th, 1960 in America.

Yvette was born at the Bryn Mawr Hospital. When they asked me for the name of our new baby girl I said, "Monique de Botton" which was a French name. My husband yelled, "No way. No Monique name!!!" It would be hard for him to hear the word at the end of Monique "Nique" which means in the Arabic language "Fuck !!!!"

So we changed our baby girl's name from "Monique" to "Yvette."

My Third Child Nicole was Born August 5th, 1967 in America.

Seven years later my second daughter Nicole was born in Lankenau Hospital. Everyone calls her by her nickname "Nique" until today. We did forget our Arabic words with the time passing and no one in America knows the real meaning of this word.

The Arab word "Nique" means.... you know what!

Paul was raised while living at the Brierhurst Hotel in a drawer. We were afraid to lay him in our bed between us because we could suffocate him. We also didn't have a crib yet. So we decided to put a blanket in our top bedroom drawer which we put on the floor next to our bed. One day, I read on the bulletin board of the lobby that a used crib was available for ten dollars which I could afford. So I got very excited and told the manager to bring the crib up to my room. When I saw the crib, it was so filthy. I thought that Claude would be furious at me so I went down to tell the manager I no longer wanted the crib. I spotted an old man painting the walls of the lobby in a white color. I asked him to come up to my room to paint the crib before my husband returned. He painted the crib and my happiness stopped when he asked me to use the bathroom. He came out naked. I was shocked. I guess he thought I was a French prostitute and he wanted to be paid with sex! Because he was an old man, it never occurred to me that it was dangerous to bring a stranger into my room. I took Paul and we ran as quickly as we could down the fire stairs. I never did report this event to Claude because he would have looked for this man to kill him! This is a nightmare that I can never forget.

When the weather was nice, I used to take Paul to the Park on 52nd street carrying him on my shoulders. We could not afford a stroller. One day, while we were sitting and playing on the grass of the park which was a fifteen minute walk from the hotel, it began to rain buckets. I started running back with Paul screaming on my shoulders. We were getting soaking wet. I knocked on someone's door to ask for help. A man opened the door and nicely asked me to come inside away from the pouring rain. I suddenly realized that if anything happened to us, no one would find us. So I quickly left and continued running under the rain until we arrived safely back. This is another nightmare I can never forget.

I started taking the train to the University of Pennsylvania with my baby Paul. We would play on the campus grass or I would give him his bottle to drink. It was just the two of us until Claude finished his classes. I remember how sad for me it was to see all those happy students, boys and girls, who were my own age (twenty-one). They passed me by in groups with their books carried under their arms. I felt invisible to them. What a difference between my lonely life at home and theirs being educated in a wonderful college.

One Sunday, when Paul was one year old, Claude took us to the beach. I was so happy to see the ocean again! While I was playing in the sand with my boy, Claude was quietly reading his book next to us. I started digging a hole in the sand and found a ten dollar bill! For me at the time it was the same as my whole weekly allowance! If I showed it to Claude, he would order me to give it back immediately to the young lifeguard sitting on his tall chair. I knew that I shouldn't keep the money. It wasn't mine. But that money which I had found at the bottom of the hole was definitely lost a long time ago. I didn't say anything to anyone and I hid it in my bathing suit when Claude wasn't looking. Paul started to cry for his bottle. So I went to heat his bottle on top of the old stove's cabin we were staying in. An explosion! Both my hands got burned. We rushed to the nearest doctor who took care of it. When he was finished, he asked us for his bill: ten dollars. Claude tried to explain that he didn't have any money to give him as we were still in our bathing suits. He was petrified. So in slow motion, I dug inside of my bathing suit and showed the ten dollars we needed to pay the doctor. Claude just couldn't believe his eyes! But he was certainly relieved! My mother always told me that in the Middle East they burnt the hands of a thief to punish him. I guess this time she was right!

Claude could not afford a car. He always took the bus or the train to go to work. I was left alone with my baby in the worst neighborhood. I couldn't speak English so I followed the soap operas on TV because the actors were my only company. I repeated what they were saying in English and repeated it loudly so I could learn the English language well. This same opera show "As The World Turns" started at 2 pm every afternoon. It was my best hour because my baby Paul was already fed and sleeping. I even took notes in French.

I kept remembering my life in Egypt, where I had graduated from Le Baccalaureat at the "Lycée Français" as a good and popular student with my teachers and my friends. Growing up at home, we had many servants to cook and serve. I lived a joyful, carefree life with my mom, dad, my brother Raymond and baby Gilbert. Also with many cousins, aunts, uncles and grandparents. But here, in America, I had to survive completely alone. I decided one day to cook a meal to surprise my husband. I boiled oil in a pan. Then I threw in cut potatoes I had prepared including the water they were soaking in. I did not know that you should never put water in boiling oil. No one told me! (A big mistake!) Wow!! A big explosion!!!! The whole kitchen took fire and when Claude arrived, he was furious at me and called me "stupid, idiot" and all the bad words I had never heard from him before!!! What happened to the Joyce of Egypt he adored, respected and admired as his queen?? The poor Joyce had turned into a stupid, uneducated, ignorant woman as his wife in America!! What had happened to the happy, popular, funny, smart Joyce??

I could not even speak English to my American son! I only spoke French to him. One day the principal of his child-care school called to tell me that my son was called "Me too" in the class. Paul, who only knew the French language had figured out to say the magical words "Me too" whenever the teacher or a classmate spoke to him. With this "Me too" response, Paul seemed to manage for a bit. They all called him by the name "Me too." The principal asked me to speak only English to my son from then on. But when I answered the principal in my broken bad English, he told me "Madame, continue to speak to your son in French and WE will teach him English!!" I felt humiliated and ignorant as I always felt in America.

My life was too lonely at home with my baby. I begged my cousin Rolande to visit me in my new place with no furniture, a baby crib and a sofa bed in the living room for her. I was praying that maybe if I introduced her to some American boy she would marry him and live in America. So I made a list of Claude's friends who were single and then set her up on a date with each one. They invited her for lunch or dinner. I used to watch her getting dressed and then I waited for her to come back, excited to hear about her time. Inside of me, I was praying for Rolande to come back as Cinderella after meeting her prince at the ball, exclaiming that she would now live forever next to me and I would have someone from my family at last in America. But to my luck, every time she returned she would tell me how much she missed her boyfriend in Brazil. She returned to Brazil and got engaged immediately to the love of her life, Sergio

Sonnino, who waited for her. When she left, I missed the time we had spent together with laughter and giggles the way best friends do.

A few months later Claude's aunt Gaby Salama, who lived in Switzerland and was divorced, came to visit us. I again made a list of Claude's single acquaintances and scheduled a new date for her every night. I prayed that after she spent time with a special man she would return happy and excited because she had found the love of her life and would live in America next to us. Again it never happened. Instead she went to New York and met, through another niece, a widower named Al Capp from Alabama who asked her to marry him. He took her back to live in Montgomery, Alabama. Yes she moved to America, but still she lived far from me. I really tried my best to keep a member of my family in Philadelphia, but it just didn't work.

Then came my first religious holiday in America. I needed to borrow a hat to attend services. In Egypt we belonged to an Orthodox Synagogue. Claude found one not too far from where we lived. I was miserable through the whole service sitting alone upstairs far from Claude, who was praying downstairs among all the men. The women close to me spoke among themselves, whispering in a low voice. They knew each other and were happy and excited to meet again for the holidays. I felt alone remembering my family's holidays at our Temple in Egypt surrounded by my family, full of joy and love. Why did this happen to me?? I wanted to leave. I was crying inside but I couldn't contact my husband who was downstairs. Later I learned that in America there were other types of synagogues where I could pray next to my husband such as the "Conservative," "Liberal" and "Reform" ones. Because in Egypt girls did not go to Hebrew school, I was very happy to follow the services at Main Line Reform temple where we prayed in English and Hebrew. Most importantly, I sat next to my husband which made me very happy.

One day Claude told me that we were going to a football game. I got excited because I knew well this sport which was the most popular sport for young boys in Egypt. As we sat down in a far away seat, looking down at all those men falling on each other continuously, I asked Claude when the football game would start. He said, "This is the game." "No way!" I said. "This is no football game because they don't kick the ball with the feet like in Egypt. This is a game of hand-ball." Claude explained that the same game we call "Football" in Egypt, is called "Soccer" in America. I was confused and thought that nothing is the same in America as it was in Egypt.

On my first visit to my parents in Brazil, my mom thought to invite me alone with her to a French dessert restaurant. I confessed to my mom that my life in America was very hard for me, alone with my baby, away from my family and my husband gone all day long. Shedding lonely tears, I burst into crying. Suddenly a man appeared to us. He wanted to know why this French young woman was crying in the arms of her mother. He introduced himself as Billy Graham, an American. He apologized that he could not speak or understand French. I recognized him as the famous American Evangelist and spoke to him in English explaining that I lived in America in Pennsylvania, USA. He told me that his daughter also lived in PA , USA raising horses. We talked the whole afternoon while my poor mom, who did not understand our English chat, wondered who this man was interrupting us? I told her in French that he was 'un evangelist tres celebre.' At the end of our conversation, as we were the last ones at the restaurant, he said he wanted to bless me in a prayer. I stopped him explaining, "I am Jewish." He still took out a paper and wrote for me a blessing signing it, 'Billy Graham.' When

I showed it to Claude, my husband put it in an envelope along with his little Mezuzah. He sealed the envelope and placed it in my wallet. This way I would be protected by both religious prayers. My children would often take the sacred envelope from my wallet and carry it to school during exams for good luck.

My happiness in America began as soon as I moved to Chetwynd Apartments in Rosemont, PA. It was here that I started to feel like I belonged in America. I made many friends with my neighbors who also had come from abroad; Maria from Italy, Helen from Poland and Felix from France. We had already met Claude's roommate from college, Howard Lidz, who helped us from the beginning in America and he became Paul's Godfather. Also Evelyn Bodek, who was Claude's boss's daughter. Evelyn became a very important friend of mine and Paul's Godmother. My friends Nori, Joan and Tanya became my Bridge card game partenaires for fifty years. At Chetwynd we used to meet everyday in summer at the resident pool. Together, we raised our children who loved playing with one another. On Halloween, we dressed them in their Halloween costumes together. They had so much fun when they were free to knock at each apartment door in the building for "Trick or Treat." It was very safe then.

There were other pregnant women like me living at Chetwynd. The husbands also got along well. My life had finished being lonely in America.

Paul was often sick with eczema. Many times I had to take him to the Children's Hospital wishing it was me in pain and not my child. He was good looking with the most beautiful blue eyes. He could not stop scratching his whole body which made it often bloody. I used to bathe him in a tub full of oatmeal. Then I would cream him and wrap his whole body with Saran Wrap. I did it with tears in my eyes.

From Paris, Claude's parents sent me their eleven year old son who was Claude's brother, Alain. We were to raise Alain and have him live with us in our little apartment. At that time, Paul was two years old and I was pregnant with Yvette. I was nauseous all the time. I raised Alain many years by myself with no one to help me clean, do laundry, cook, and take care of my family. I slept very little and I was very tired. Yvette was born on July 30th, 1960. She was the cutest, adorable little baby who always was smiling, loving and easy to care for. I was only twenty-three years old. I enjoyed dressing her up in girl's clothes. Her brother Paul was always hugging her and protecting her. And the best thing for me was that my mom came to help me with my newborn baby. It was her first visit to America and I hadn't seen her for years!! She stayed with us a whole month sharing with me all the work I used to do by myself. When she left to go back to Brazil, I cried because I was going to miss the help and love she had given us all while she was staying with us. Claude had been spoiled by her cooking and caring and Paul was missing his "Guine" very much. I was again separated from my family. I felt more alone when she was gone.

Moving From Place To Place.

We decided to move to Balwyn, a duplex apartment which Claude had built for his boss at the time, Mr. Bodek. It had two floors. We lived on the first floor and on the floor above us lived a woman who worked at night and slept in the day. She could hear my kids play and she would bang her broom on the floor to let us know that she needed to sleep. Paul and Yvette could not make any noise in the day or they would hear the ceilings shake. It was hard for me to keep my children from playing at home.

We moved to a new building across the street. It was called "Park City West." It was again an apartment building with lots of friends and it also had a swimming pool. We were all very happy and the children would ride the elevators freely to visit their friends or go to the pool by themselves. While living in Park City West, Alain met his wife, Evelyne. He brought her home and introduced her to us before marrying her.

I became pregnant with Nicole and gave her birth on August 5th,1967 at Lankenau Hospital. She was a beautiful baby. She was the love and joy of our home. I gave a sister to Yvette, which I myself never had. Paul and Yvette couldn't stop fighting to hold her. I was very scared that they would drop her one day. She slept often in the same bed between her brother and sister.

Soon after we added two dogs (Boxers from England) into the apartment. Our Boxer named "Lady" became the children's favorite pet. The apartment became too small for us with our dogs, so Claude built for us our own home that we called "Chantilly." But when we moved into our new home, the kids hated it. They had lost their freedom of riding the elevators by themselves to visit the many friends they had made in the building. Most of all, they hated sleeping in separate rooms when they were used to sleeping together in the same bed. We never found them sleeping in their own room. They complained and wanted to go back to Park City West Apartments. What a disappointment for Claude. He thought he had built our dream house!!!

One day Claude announced that we had a visitor named Ronnie Rubin coming to our home to speak to him about a possible business partnership. While he was talking to Claude, I noticed the big difference in their clothes. Ronnie was wearing a trim fitting suit with a slim tie and a handkerchief in his pocket. He was the same size and height as Claude. I looked at my husband, who was still wearing his loose fitting suit made in Egypt with big lapels and a large tie. He looked like a villager in comparison. At one point, Ronnie suggested I meet his wife named Marcia because he thought we would get along well. When Ronnie left I told Claude "My love, I don't need to meet his wife. I need you to meet his tailor and it is time that you buy new American clothes."

While living in the suburbs, we formed a very fun group made up of the Rubins (who are until now our best friends), the Cohns (Suzanne Cohn also suffered and survived World War II when she was young in Poland), the Nipons, the Rosens, the Grosses, the Strausses, the Goldsteins and the Silvermans. We met Freddy and Monette Robinson with whom we spent the best times of our lives. Our children Paul and Cary are still best friends, as are Paul and the Gross' eldest son Andrew, and they have all continued the next generation's friendships until now. I had another group of girls called the "Hanky Pankys" with Faye, Marlene and Jill. Faye invited us many times to Arizona in her beautiful home. In later years, Charlie and Inger Sexton became Claude's and my best traveling companions around the world. Their friendship was a turning point in my life.

It was my happiest time in America with my wonderful husband and my beautiful three children surrounded by close friends who remained my best friends until now.

I want to share a story about my three children. Because I loved being a ballerina in Egypt, I decided to send Yvette to ballet school in America. She preferred Modern and Jazz dances, and she danced them for years. Then when I sent Nicole to ballet school, she hated it and made sure to forget her ballet shoes every time. I gave up. It was a big surprise for me when my college son Paul told me that he was dying to take ballet lessons!! I couldn't believe it! He would be wearing a tutu on his toes! He calmed me down by telling me that all sports people use the discipline of ballet to control their steps. He took a semester of ballet and loved it! That was funny for me! It was my son and not my daughters who had inherited my passion for ballet!!

Bridal Shower in America.

My mother had told me that the worst time for a bride is the night before her wedding when she has to go through a cleansing ritual. (I did not know then that this ritual bath for brides which was called the "Mikhail Bath" was a Jewish tradition in Egypt.) She told me how horrible it was for her as a young bride to have been laying naked in a bathtub with people watching. Horrified, she had closed her eyes the whole time.

One day, Claude told me that a student at school was getting married and that his future bride was inviting me to her Shower before the marriage. I figured out that in America all was made faster and modernized. I thought that instead of being invited to watch her naked in the bathtub, I would be watching her naked in a shower!!! I guess it was the American way for this ritual my mom went through. I didn't want to go and watch her suffering like my mom did before her marriage. I didn't even know her!!! I threw away the Shower invitation and refused to go. Later, when I was asked why I had missed the Shower, I answered anxiously "Was the bride naked?" Surprised by my question, they explained to me that a Bridal Shower in America is a fun lunch with many presents for the bride. I understood then that a Shower in America was not at all what I thought it was.

My First Vacation in America.

I was invited to take a trip with my new friend named Nori who was the gym teacher at the St. Joseph Academy. Because all the other teachers were nuns at the school, she was asked to chaperone the senior class on their trip to the Ocean City beach in New Jersey. Nori invited me to come along. It was the best treat for me. The trip was free and I had never traveled anywhere since arriving in America. The school girls were nineteen years old, the same age as I was when I got married in Egypt. I looked younger than they did because I wasn't wearing any makeup. Also, they knew how to sleep with rollers in their hair. They looked beautiful, mature and ready for a great evening. One time, I heard one of them say to her friend, "Every time she opens her mouth she puts her foot in it!!!" I could not believe what I had heard. I approached them and asked them "Why is she doing this? Is she an acrobat? It must be very difficult to put a foot in a mouth!" They started laughing at me, repeating my question with a french accent. Sadly, I did not know why they were laughing. I felt so stupid when they explained to me that this is just an English expression.

We chaperoned the girls to a dancing place and I watched them drinking, smoking and dancing while celebrating their freedom. In Egypt I had not been allowed to date or go dancing until I met Claude. He took me dancing for a very short time and then he left for America. I waited for him at home. When he came back there was the war. Here in America, I was shy and I had never danced before with strangers. So, when some boys asked me to dance (though my feet were dying to join them and dance), I answered "I am sorry sir. I can't dance with you because I am married!" I heard them laugh at me and pointing their fingers at me while repeating in a funny accented voice like mine, "She is married!!! No, no no!!" I felt ashamed and wanted to hide. I watched those young people who were having so much fun dancing the Twist. I stood against a wall, alone, watching them as a chaperone should do. My feet wanted to dance. I decided to escape to the empty 'toilettes' and I danced the Twist alone in front of the mirror while I could still hear the sound of the music playing outside. Then I cried for the comparison of this evening I had witnessed, and how it contrasted with my lonely life at home. I was twenty-one years old.

CHAPTER 13

First Jobs in America.

MY YOUNG CHILDREN GO TO SCHOOL. I NEED TO WORK.

My First Job.

But what could I do with my broken English and my strong French accent?

I asked my husband if he had any connection with the chic most important store in Philadelphia called "Nan Duskin." I thought that I could maybe work in the store as a seller of French perfumes or French designer clothes like Chanel or Christian Dior. I got so excited when Claude told me it was done and the store appointment was at 9 am the next morning. So I went well prepared with my hair up in a French twist. I also wore my high heels and put on my best makeup. I looked French. At 9 am someone was waiting for me at the entrance of Nan Duskin and I gave my French name "Jocelyne De Botton." I did look very elegant with a big smile on my face! The lady took me straight to the basement and showed me my work: I had to empty all day long those big boxes filled with dresses of all sizes and hang each one up on a bar with a hanger, separating them size by size. An eight year old girl could have done this!!! I graduated in Egypt in Philosophy, I spoke French, Arabic and a little bit of every Mediteranean language!! What was I doing working here in the store's basement?

When lunchtime came, all the girls had their own lunches prepared in bags. They were eating together, laughing and speaking

English. I was hungry and my high heels were killing me! I looked at them and they were all wearing sneakers! I went to the bathroom, locked myself in and cried quite a few times. When Claude came back at 5 pm to pick me up, I wanted to kill myself or kill him!! My first work in America was a disaster.

My Second Job in America.

I decided to use my languages to help people. So I joined the Tourist Bureau in town, the "VIP" office. This is where people came who only spoke French or Arabic, and who wanted to tour Philadelphia with explanations in their own languages. I loved it!! I was so happy and so proud. Everyday when my kids were in school, I took the train to town and worked happily because I was helping families, all tourists who couldn't understand English well!! I became popular at the office and even was given a medal!!

One day, a young and handsome Arab asked me if I could help him with his real estate trip to Washington. He also asked me if I could help him meet a Philadelphia real estate builder. I would be the translator. Well, I thought to myself that I knew exactly who he needed to meet! My husband!

I took him straight to meet him at his office. Claude politely answered the man's business questions. Just when I was leaving the office, Claude murmured in my ears "Enjoy your last day at work!" I had made a big mistake to take that handsome tourist with me to the office. My husband, being a true Middle Eastern man, hated to see me spend the day alone with a man. It was indeed the last day at a job which made me so happy and proud for helping all of those non-English speaking tourists who needed me.

One day, I happened to meet the famous boxer Muhammad Ali at the department store. I taught him how to write his name in Arabic since he had now become a Muslim! He then gratefully offered to drive me home in his car. I answered him, "Driving me home will be dangerous for you. You will be punched 'knockout' fast when my husband sees you at the door with me!"

At the airport one day, as I was waiting with Paul and Yvette for Claude to bring back the car from the garage, an old, fat man standing next to me started bombarding me with many questions. It was very clear that he annoyed me. I didn't answer him and was rude to him by stepping a few steps away. When Claude drove back and saw the man, he exclaimed loudly "Joyce, that's Alfred Hitchcock who is talking to you!!" I turned around and I asked the fat man if he was really the famous movie producer. He smiled at me and I felt guilty for having treated the great Alfred Hitchcock so badly!

Another time, the famous French singer Charles Aznavour (like our Frank Sinatra) came to our house. When he started to sing to me, my husband left to bring him his umbrella and his raincoat. He told him that they had to leave because it was getting too late to drive him back under the rain. Can you imagine if one of your favorite singers came to your house and started to sing to you and was interrupted to have to leave??!!!

Third Job Which Lasted Over Ten Years.

After many unsuccessful jobs, my husband offered me to work at his own office for his real estate firm called "National Realty Corporation." What a pity that I could not use my knowledge of different languages at his office!! At 9 am we drove to his office at 1604 Walnut Street. When we arrived, he called one of his secretaries named Ethel and told her to take care of me for my first day at the office. Indeed she did!! She got me a bunch of envelopes, pages of hundreds of stamps and a little sponge with water. My work was set to stick one stamp at a time on each envelope all day long!! Again, I was humiliated to have been given such an eight year old simple task. I went to lunch with the other secretaries. At 5 o'clock, I cried on my return ride home with my boss, my husband. I swore to him that there was no more office work for me!! He begged me to come back one more day. The next day at 9 am we arrived at the office and went straight to the big conference table where the office staff was sitting and waiting for the boss. He announced to all, "I present you the new Vice President!!" (ME the Vice President?) !!!! It sure was a way to demand respect from everyone working with me now.

I worked in my own office for years as the Public Relations Vice President. I used all the major newspapers to advertise National Realty Corporation's properties.

My husband was my boss at the office and my boss at home. Then my son Paul, who had joined National Realty Corporation, gave me his own orders. When my baby Nicole joined the company, she started to give me her recommendations to begin advertising online and on the computer. (I didn't have any idea how to do it). I thought, no way!! Nicole was right, the future of advertisement was online.

I had worked at the office already for almost ten years. I was proud that I contributed to the success of the Real Estate business. I am proud to say that I was good as Vice President of Public Relations.

I was also responsible for the hiring of the new employees for the company. At the office I used to see my boss (my husband), close the door so he could quietly dictate his orders to one secretary at a time. I worked in my room alone and I was not allowed to interrupt them. So I decided that the girls I hired would be older and homely. The pretty ones didn't have a chance! One day my girlfriend Marlene Dubin came to the office to pick me up for lunch. She told me that she thought she was visiting a nursing home. I told her proudly that they were chosen by the boss's wife! I loved each one of them and always enjoyed going to lunch with them. But when Nicole took over the company... the office staff turned into a model agency!!

CHAPTER 14

Our Summer and Winter Vacations.

PAPI AND I TOOK ALL OF OUR CHILDREN AND GRAND-children every year on different vacations. Cruises were the best. But anywhere we went we had so much fun together. I hope that they have kept the many memories of our family trips. If they did happen to forget, I have in my albums thousands of pictures to remind my loved ones.

Because Raymond and his daughter Carina live in London and because Gilbert and his daughter Evelyn live in Brazil and because of me, who lives in America with my family, we have always been separated, the three of us by living in three different countries. But we have managed to love and meet each other as often as we can.

I was lucky to be able to travel many times to Brazil to visit my parents. It was such a wonderful time with the whole family spoiling me with their love. We went together to their beach houses in Guaruja. We spent fun times with all my cousins and my aunts. I am still very close to my cousins Rolande, Daisy, Lody, Rosita and Rozelyn. I adored my aunts, "Tante" Paula, "Tante" Henriette and "Tante" Marcelle. I flew to Brazil in the winter which was summer there. Raymond always joined me from London. In America I missed them too much.

Nicole and Yvette lived at their Uncle Raymond's home in London during their college Junior year abroads. They were served by his butler! Our three children, Paul, Yvette and Nicole loved visiting my family on their winter vacation at their grandparents' Guine and grandpa Salvo's beach home. The December month is the summer month in Brazil. They played racquets on the sand and swam in the clear warm ocean. They were always surrounded by aunts, uncles and cousins who adored them. It was so special for me to have my children having fun and loving my family though they grew up far away in America.

In summers we went to Cannes in the south of France to spend our vacation with Claude's family. It was a very special time for us to live at "Meme and Dada's" home including Alain's family, who were all living in England. We loved sailing with the whole family on their boat named "Sparklet."

Later, Claude and I sailed through the South of France on Raymond's boat named "Just for You" with Carina, our mom (Guine), Gilbert, Evelyne and Rolande. We have sailed together from Nice to Corsica and to Sardinia. Summers were great for us! They started first in our own summer beach place in Ventnor, New Jersey called "The Sands" while our children went to their favorite summer camps in the Poconos. After or before camps, our pool at home was everyone's favorite place. In later years, my grandchildren especially enjoyed playing together in the pool and the jacuzzi with all the toys I surprised them with. They also loved racing in the pool with their Papi and swimming in my arms or swinging on the hammock with their cousins.

We spent our winter vacations in Brazil or in Acapulco, or in our favorite family spot in Dorado, Puerto Rico. They were beautiful and warm places that reminded me of my summers in Egypt. I remember that those winter vacations were the best for my son Paul who suffered from a serious eczema all over his body each winter. The minute he got to the sun his eczema disappeared. I was so relieved to see him jumping in the ocean with his sisters, delivered from his pain finally.

CHAPTER 15

My Charities as Chairman of Events.

STILL WANTING TO WORK, I CHOSE TO PRODUCE SUC-
cessful events to raise money for charities. My best events were
when I gave the most extraordinary ball at the Franklin Institute of
Philadelphia for "Juvenile Diabetes," and another one even more successful for the charity called "Tay Sachs" (which I had never heard
of). It was a charity for the disease that only Ashkenazi Jews could
get and I was Safardic.

For each charity I was able to raise a big amount of money
by selecting very important guests to be honored: Mademoiselle
De Mazia, who was my teacher at the Barnes Foundation where I
took lessons for years; Mr. Mondavi, who came from California (the
owner of the American Mondavi wines); Ricardo Muti, the great
conductor who brought the whole Philadelphia Orchestra to play for
us, and many more famous people to honor at the balls. My daughter Yvette surprised me and everyone by singing Barbra Streisand's
song "You don't bring me flowers anymore" with the Philadelphia
Orchestra. The audience thought for a moment that she was Barbra
Streisand singing!

At the Juvenile Diabetes Super Achievers Ball at the Franklin
Institute Museum, I made a welcoming speech. "This ball for me is
like having a baby. It took me nine full months to prepare it. Well,
tonight the baby is born! And I thank my husband, Claude, the man
of my life, my long suffering mate. "Honey, Cherie, it is all over!"
And Claude responded, "Nice to have her back again!"

All the top local newspapers wrote that these charity balls were the best ones ever given and that they raised the most money. I made my family proud of me.

Soon after, I became a speaker when I was asked to tell my story as a Jewish girl born, raised and married in an Arab country.

I was now a proud citizen in America!!!!

CHAPTER 16

I Met Madame Jehan El Sadat, Wife of the Ex-President of Egypt, Anwar El Sadat.

NABILA, MY HIGH SCHOOL FRIEND IN ALEXANDRIA, SUR-prised me when she called me from New York where she was living at that time. We hadn't seen each other for years!! I asked her how she found my number in Philadelphia? She responded, "Don't you remember that you left your phone number and your address during one of your visits to our school in Alexandria?"

She invited me to spend a few days with her in Washington at the Egyptian Embassy. It was here that her sister lived because her sister's husband, Ashraf Gorbal, was the Egyptian Ambassador in Washington. Here I was, the first Jew sleeping in the Egyptian Embassy in Washington!! Me, a refugee who left Egypt exiled!!

Well, the best gift for me was meeting Jehan Sadat, the wife of the late President of Egypt! It seemed that we were both guests at the Embassy. We developed a great friendship away from the public. She later came to have lunch with my family at my house in Penn Valley. She is a beautiful woman inside and outside! I am a big fan of hers and I admire her a lot. She then invited me to visit Egypt with my family. What a trip back to our birth land! Many years ago we had run away by the back door and now we were invited to return through the main door, the palace.

She welcomed us in Cairo with limousines waiting at the airport and big flower arrangements at every hotel she put us in. She invited my family to her Sadat's residence and she was the best hostess, showing us her home and telling my children Paul, Yvette and Nicole (she was fifteen at that time) how she met the future President of Egypt, Anwar Sadat. At fifteen, she met him in prison and fell madly in love despite the fact that he was a prisoner and very poor.

With my family, we then visited our homes in Alexandria, our schools and our temple. Every place had changed. While driving by a photography store Paul exclaimed, "Mom, isn't that your picture in the window?" I could not believe that a picture that had been taken of me when I was fifteen years old, was the only picture used to advertise the store called "My Studio." Papi immediately went inside and tried to buy my photo from the owner, who first made it difficult to do until Papi paid a big price. When we asked our Arab driver, "How can we possibly describe the beautiful Alexandria of the past that we knew?" he answered, "I still can not describe to my own children the beautiful Alexandria of the past when all you Jews lived here among us…" It was definitely a very emotional trip for us.

A few years later, Pennsylvania Senator Arlen Specter called me from Washington and asked me for a favor: He needed to meet, as soon as possible, my friend Mrs. Sadat. I called her immediately and she agreed to meet the Pennsylvania Senator and me for lunch the same day. It was the summer of 1990 and I flew to Washington from Atlantic City where I was at the time. At lunch, the senator asked her if her late husband had known Saddam Hussein of Iraq. He told her that he was just returning from a mission in Iraq where he had interviewed Saddam Hussein and had asked him if he was ever going to invade Kuwait. In the interview Saddam Hussein promised America that he would never invade this Kuwait. Before reporting Saddam's promise to President George W. Bush, the senator wanted to know her thoughts about Saddam Hussein. Jehan answered that they did know Saddam Hussein very well as the biggest liar. They could never trust him. She said, "My husband thought of Saddam as the man who could never be trusted. If Saddam promised America never to invade Kuwait, he was definitely preparing an invasion of Kuwait right now and America should be ready."

She was right. Saddam Hussein had lied to the senator and he did invade Kuwait soon after. Thank God Specter changed his report to President Bush according to Mrs Sadat's words. America got ready for the Gulf War with a massive U.S. offensive attack known as "Operation Desert Storm." Later Specter told me that he would never stop thanking me for my help that day. He would have given the President the wrong report. I felt that because of my friendship with Mrs. Sadat that I had become part of the American history.

CHAPTER 17

My Project for Peace.

YASSER ARAFAT, THE PALESTINIAN LEADER OF PLO fought with terrorism killing thousands of people in Israel. He was given the Nobel Peace prize in 1994!! It was a big mistake, very hard to believe, but why? He certainly did not deserve it.

In Washington, in 1979, Egyptian President Anwar Sadat traveled courageously to Israel to meet Israel Prime Minister Menachem Begin. Together these leaders signed a peace treaty between their two nations. Standing in between them was U.S. President Jimmy Carter who officiated it.

Looking at those three men who were joining hands for peace made me emotional and I cried tears of joy. These three men who were signing peace represented my own peace.

Sadat- I was born in Egypt, my birth land.

Begin - My Jewish religion.

Carter - My American citizenship!!

I was so happy and proud!! It was a miracle! I never thought it could ever happen!!

President Anwar Sadat was shot and killed in Cairo in 1981. This was only a couple of years later. He was assassinated by an Egyptian Fundamentalist army officer during the annual Victory Parade.

Meanwhile Yitzhack Rabin, the Israel Prime Minister was also shot by one of his men. He was killed in Tel Aviv after a peace rally. Rabin and Sadat were both killed in their own countries by their own people because of their desire for peace.

Lea Rabin (Israel)　　　　　*Jehan Sadat (Egypt)*

One day I woke up with a new idea for peace. With both the Egyptian and the Israeli Presidents assassinated in their own countries by their own people while trying to make peace, why not let their widows continue their mission of peace? Why not have Jehan Sadat and Lea Rabin become "Ambassadors of Peace" in the Middle East? Two women who want to spare the Egyptian and Israeli children and grandchildren from unnecessary wars!!! Women could be better at diplomacy for peace. Do not let Arafat dictate wars again! I worked hard at this idea. Women could be better than men at stopping wars in the world.

When I visited Egypt with my family, I talked to Egyptian students and to my Egyptian friends about the idea to name Lea Rabin and Jehan Sadat "Ambassadors of Peace." They all confirmed that my idea was the best. I contacted my temple and other synagogues. I contacted Hadassah plus all the Jewish women organizations in America and they all liked my idea. Everyone was excited and ready to support the project. First I spoke to my friend Jehan Sadat. Then I contacted Pennsylvania Senator Arlen Specter and also Marjorie Margolies (now Chelsea's mother-in-law). I asked her to contact her friend Hillary Clinton who was then the U.S. First Lady. She told me that Mrs. Clinton was very interested in participating. Lastly, I sent the message to Lea Rabin through my friend Felix Zandman, a very good friend of hers. While in Israel, he contacted Leah and explained to her that women can help peace better than anyone. Leah was my last one to answer but Felix called me back from Israel to give me the sad news. No one knew yet that Lea Rabin was sick. Mrs. Rabin told Felix that even though she liked the idea that she would not be able to do it. She died soon after and my dream died with her!!

Well, I thought that I could make a difference. I tried and it almost happened!

CHAPTER 18

I Am an American.

MORE THAN SIXTY YEARS IN AMERICA, AND PEOPLE meeting me and hearing me speak would still ask me, "Where do you come from?" I would answer, "I am from Philadelphia" and they would say, "No, before? Where are you coming from?" "I am American!!!" "No, before America?" "I was born in Alexandria, Egypt." "Are you then an Egyptian Arab?" "No, I am a Jewish American!!" "So why does your accent sound French?" "Because we used to talk French and Arabic in Egypt!!"

So no matter what, I still sounded like a foreigner all my life. I had three American children: Paul Mario de Botton born in 1958, Yvette Fortunée de Botton born in 1960, and my baby Nicole Evelyne de Botton born in 1967. Their middle names, Mario, Fortunee and Evelyne are the same as our still alive parents' names whom they met and loved. This is the Sephardic tradition which is opposite to the Ashkenazi that names children and grandchildren after grandparents that have passed away. As my birth name is "Jocelyne," I have four of our granddaughters with their middle name "Jocelyne": Alessandra Jocelyne, Michelle Jocelyne, Brooke Lilly Jocelyne, and Danielle Sidney Jocelyne. Our granddaughter, Claudia de Botton has Papi's name, Claude de Botton. For the boys, we have Will de Botton Robinson, Michael Claude de Botton and Jack Ira Claude Robinson.

No one will ask them where they came from the way they always asked me.

CHAPTER 19

We Did Not Say Goodbye.

IT HAD BEEN FORTY YEARS SINCE WE HAD LEFT OUR girls' school in Alexandria "Le Lycée Français." We met again in Paris after a lot of work trying to locate each other. The big problem for us was that our single girls' names had changed to our married names. No one had said where they were flying to when exiled from Egypt. No one had said goodbye before running away.

When we met again, it was an impossible dream for us. I made a speech: "Forty years ago we were seventeen years old, from the same school, the same town, wearing the same clothes of young Egyptian girls. Today we meet as wives, mothers and grandmothers. Some of us adopted their new country like Italy or France or Spain, Israel, Belgium or Brazil, where my parents live now. I live in America with my husband Claude de Botton (also born in Egypt) and my three children. We are different now, living in different worlds, different cultures, different friends and different dreams. All those years in Egypt, I never knew that some of you were Greek or Algerian or Jewish or Christians or Muslims. We used to be one. We got along with each other and we respected one another. We were all the same living in our Alexandria. We visited each other's home and we had freedom of religion. Then we became separated because of a sudden war and we left Egypt because it didn't want us anymore. But it is a miracle to meet again, here in Paris, an impossible dream for all of us. Now we are back together, sharing our students' past history and sharing our pictures, sharing our forty years of old stories since we last saw each other. We shall end this reunion in Paris saying "Goodbye" and we shall remain in contact from now on."

P.S. I had heard each one of their sad stories about leaving Egypt as refugees with no money, about going to different possible countries and how hard it was for them to start again. Similar to my own beginnings in America the stories were very sad, and also spoke of loneliness and pain at being separated from family and friends. But there was a difference to our exile story. The American people had welcomed me warmly with open arms. They had accepted me and had given me love and friendship when I met them.

I returned home and I told Claude that we had been so lucky to come and live in America!!! I was feeling proud of my new country.

"JE SUIS HEUREUSE."

We met in Paris in 1995 and we did say goodbye.

CHAPTER 20

Our 60th Wedding Anniversary.

AT CLAUDE AND MY 60TH WEDDING ANNIVERSARY, OUR children organized an unbelievable ceremony for us in Palm Springs, California. It was a very emotional time for us.

Our children had found a California rabbi to bless us. They chose a romantic place to hold the ceremony that was outside against a cascade of falling water. When we walked hand in hand to the music "Here comes the bride," I was wearing a white bridal gown and I couldn't stop shedding tears of joy! Our children and grandchildren were waiting for us, seated in a circle facing the rabbi. Each one then stood up and came towards us holding a flower which they placed at our feet along with a blessing. This was followed by a delicious dinner. Then our ten grandchildren sang a song they had written for us and gave speeches. There was the clinking of glasses followed by a beautiful wedding cake.

This magical wedding celebration replaced our sad wedding in Egypt sixty years ago.

CHAPTER 21

My Family's Achievements in America.

CLAUDE NEEDED TO HAVE A JOB TO MAKE MONEY TO take care of us. He asked Shelly Gordon, his fraternity friend at Penn, if someone could help him find a job. Shelly told him to call his father-in-law, Ralph Bodek.

Mr. Ralph Bodek was a builder in Delaware County. Claude started working as an office boy. At the time, there was no fax, no emails, and no printing. Claude brought and took things to and from Mr. Bodek's lawyers, bankers and architects. He learned a lot from this job because Mr. Bodek got drunk in the mornings but before he got drunk, he gave Claude his orders for the day. Claude obediently followed the orders completely on his own.

One day Mr. Bodek asked Claude to design the new houses he would build in Marple Township, Delaware County. Claude was the first in Pennsylvania who changed the design of houses. He replaced the garage with a big den and a bathroom. He gave the buyer the choice between the old design or the new one. It was a big success in Delaware County because it was the first of its kind in the community. At the time, Claude was only twenty-five years old.

After his work, Claude came home where I became his first secretary because he couldn't afford one. He would dictate notes to me to review and keep. Though I was very proud to do it, he often got angry and impatient with me because I was slow and my English was not perfect. I also didn't know shorthand and he was talking too fast to me. Together, we designed the logo "NRC" for his future company called National Realty Corporation. He also built for Mr. Bodek, all by himself, Balwyn Park Duplexes (it's still there) and Balwyn Park Shopping Center. He then left Mr. Bodek and started to build on his own.

Our Children and Grandchildren Work in America.

Our children could not join the business of NRC before being tested and having some kind of experience first in the real estate business. Paul started to work in summers during his college years. He dug ditches all day long with the construction workers. He used to complain to me that he was educated in economics and finances at the University of Pennsylvania but his father gave him a very hard job which he was not trained for and he hated it!! I explained to him that his father was preparing him for the future. I compared him to a conductor in an orchestra who has to learn first every instrument playing in the orchestra so he could be ready to lead the music with that knowledge. Paul later worked with every different team that was a part of NRC.

Nicole worked after college in London for a friend of uncle Raymond. It was a real estate investment company where she was trained to learn about the real estate business before joining NRC.

As for all of you, our grandchildren, not one of you has been allowed to join NRC until now. You have all graduated from different universities (not Dani yet) and have found your own wings to fly away and gain your independence. You are successful on your own. You have made us very proud of your accomplishments.

The Veterans Memorial and the Hall of Prayers in Newtown Square.

Due to all of Claude's success, he wanted to give back to the community and to the country that became our home. His dream and his vision for years was to build a Veterans Memorial in Delaware County. This building was very important to the community and to Claude. Nicole helped her father manage it. She especially helped with the writings on the columns where it is written the history of every American war. Claude then made the sight bigger by adding a "Hall of Prayers" for the POWs including a center empty chair waiting for the soldiers to return home. Today, he has the hopes and dreams of expanding with a Veterans Museum and more.

CHAPTER 22

The American Dream.

NOW AT EIGHTY-FIVE YEARS OLD, PAPI IS STILL DREAM-ing, building and developing everyday. He has been lucky to be helped every step of the way by his children. He always repeated to me that he could not have made it without Paul, Nicole and Rob who are working tirelessly at NRC especially now to solve all the problems that the Coronavirus has created since March of 2020 As president of NRC, Paul has inherited its many responsibilities which he shares with Nicole and Rob. They work together to ensure its continued success and growth. Paul is a very strong negotiator. He is very popular and he has many friends who love him. He is very active in the Young Presidents Organization (YPO). Nicole, after spending time in London, returned home and took on the responsibility of the renovation and running of the Willings at Independence Park. Now as Vice President, she has her hands in every division of the company including the building of the Veterans Memorial and the programming of educational events held there. Christopher (Yvette's husband), oversaw the management of the apartments in Upper Darby. He was also an integral member of the Coventry Woods Homes building team where he specialized in customizing the units. He is currently completing his painting degree at PAFA. Rob Langer (Nicole's husband), later joined the company as a leasing agent. He assists Paul in all facets of the business and like Nicole, he is involved in its everyday problems or successes. Andrea (Paul's wife), works as

Interior Designer of the Willings and the upcoming new homes in Delaware County.

Yvette, known as Yvette Om, teaches yoga and travels the country where she is invited to sing Kirtans. Her name Yvette (Yvetteom. com) is well known online as she has produced 5 CDs of her music. Every month of May she performs for thousands of people doing yoga outside on the steps of the Philadelphia Museum of Art. What an amazing sight!! This event called "Reach & Raise" takes place annually to raise money for breast cancer, a great cause.

Each one of our children has made us proud parents in America.

My Grandmothers and Strange Dreams / The Circle of Life.

I dreamt of my Abuelita telling me she loved me. I got up on February 12th, 1976 and I told Claude that I was leaving to go to Brazil that same night to see my grandmother. He could not understand why because she was not sick. He begged me to stay and go after spending Valentine's Day with him just a couple of days later. I do not know why, but I did not listen and instead I booked my plane ticket for the same night. I arrived in Brazil the next day on February 13th and I ran fast to see my grandmother. The family was very surprised to see me because I had been there a few months earlier. I went straight to my Abuelita who was blind and didn't expect me. I rested my head on her lap and as she was caressing my long, straight hair I asked her in French, "Abuelita qui je suis?" (who am I?) She answered as in a dream, "Non, impossible!!! Est ce ma jolie petite fille américaine?" We laughed full of joy to be together again and we hugged with lots of love. She used to tell me, "When you are upset, close your eyes for a few moments and all you see is black like I do. Then open your eyes, look around you and think of me who will never see. Realize the miracle of being able to see colors and people you love... how lucky you are." The next morning she died suddenly in her bed. I called Claude and said, "Happy Valentine's Day my love. Today is a very sad day for me because Abuelita just died this morning, (February 14th). I am crying right here, next to her, and tomorrow I shall attend her funeral in Brazil with all my family." My husband was not mad at me anymore.

Another time, I dreamt that my grand-maman (my dad's mom) had died in Israel. I woke up and announced to Claude that my grandmother had just died. Not believing my dream, he called my parents in Brazil who told us that today was indeed my grandmother's funeral in Israel. They could not believe that I knew it already! I guess I was spiritually connected from far away to both my grandmothers, whom I adored.

Papi's 85th Birthday.

We were lucky to celebrate Papi's eighty-fifth birthday in December of 2019 just before the Coronavirus. We were twenty-one family members! We all met in a spa in Florida. Some of us started each morning with exercise at the gym or on the golf course. Others ran to the beach for some sunbathing and swimming in the ocean. At night we gathered at the dinner table and we told our story of how we had spent the day. The last night together was at his birthday dinner which we celebrated in a specially decorated room. There was a violinist who played Claude's favorite songs. We sang and danced. There was so much love in the room for Papi.

The Coronavirus in America and all over the world.

The Coronavirus which started in China is until now killing people around the world. It is indeed a tragedy. My granddaughter who lives in New York, Claudia, has had to delay her wedding to AJ O'leary for a whole year. Michelle and Jack did not get their proper graduations. Michelle, from Elon University and Jack, from the Shipley High School. What a disappointment for them. Alessandra, who was just married before Corona to Joey Pitkow, has had to work for Comcast from her apartment online. Ariela, who moved to Boston, worked at Harvard University. But when her boss was arrested as a spy for China, her office closed. Will and Brooke have had to return home from their Junior years abroad where they both were in Australia having an amazing time. Alycia and Michael have had to return home from both their universities, completing the year online; Alycia from University of Wisconsin and Michael from Penn State. Dani, the youngest, has also had to complete her junior year of high school at Harrington online.

Because of the Coronavirus, each one of you has had to return home. We are separated and we can only meet virtually by ZOOM. Everything has stopped. Not only in America, but all over the world. I think that the Coronavirus is worse than wars.

When will it end? It is quite scary. What has happened to my beautiful and strong America? Protesters everywhere. The crowds in the streets are huge and angry.

I believe that because I went through a couple of wars in my beautiful Egypt, that now I am more frightened for the future of America. I pray that it will all pass very soon and that looking back you will think of it as just a storm that came and passed long ago in America.

For so many years, I had missed my family who had left Egypt at the same time as I did. Unlike me, they all moved together to Brazil. They had a happy life on the beach with lots of family gatherings on weekends and on holiday vacations. I lived without any of them and I was envious of all the people who could visit their families close to them. I suffered from those separations and missed my family terribly. So many times I found myself dreaming of my happy childhood when I was surrounded by their joy and their love for me. I was afraid to be forgotten from so far away. This is when I started my photography habit. I began taking pictures and sending them to all of my family in Brazil. This way my family would get to know my children growing up. I used to say to my kids, "You gave your children what I could never give you. You gave them grandparents, aunts, uncles, cousins all living around you. You called my friends by the names "Uncle Ronnie" or "Aunt Monette" or "Aunt Marcia" to replace them."

Our son Paul gave us five grandchildren: Alessandra, Ariel, Claudia, Michael and Danielle de Botton. Yvette gave us two grandchildren: Michelle and Alycia Pecoraro. Nicole gave us three grandchildren: Will, Brooke and Jack Robinson. I am also lucky to have three of my married children's wonderful mates!: Andrea de Botton, Christopher Pecoraro and Rob Langer, who added two more grandchildren, Jake and Maggie.

I am a lucky woman at the age of eighty-two. I am surrounded by an amazing family. Most of all, I am still married to Claude, my loving husband of sixty-three years whom I adore, your own Papi.

I have lived the American Dream!!

I wish you all health, happiness, success, no matter where you go. Most importantly, you should always love and support each other, as the saying goes, "United we stand. Divided we fall."

I hope that my story will teach you about your heritage and mostly about your roots which started in Egypt.

Just know that it is because of all of you that I consider myself lucky and I can repeat the French words,

"JE SUIS HEUREUSE."

Your Nana

All our children and all our grandchildren

Celebrated Claude's 85th Birthday December 2019

From bottom left: Will, Jack & Brooke Robinson, Ariel, Dani &
Michael de Botton From mid left: Christopher & Yvette Pecoraro,
Nana, Papi, Andrea & Paul de Botton From top left: Andrew Wood,
Michelle & Alycia Pecoraro, Nicole & Rob Langer, Joey & Alessandra
Pitkow, AJ & Claudia O'leary

ACKNOWLEDGEMENT

THIS BOOK HAS BEEN MY IMPOSSIBLE DREAM FOR MANY years. It has finally happened with the help of my daughter, Yvette Pecoraro, whom I could not have done this book without. She has spent many hours checking it to make sure it was well written. She signed me up with the Publishers Bookbaby and made it happen for me. Thank you to my granddaughter Brooke Robinson, who was the first to start typing my handwritten stories and who designed the beautiful front cover. Thank you to my granddaughter Michelle Pecoraro, who edited and was responsible for the choosing and placement of the book photos. Lastly, thank you to my beloved husband for allowing me time away from him to write. This has been a miracle for me. A dream comes true.

For any questions or further interest in her story
the author can be contacted at: Joagami@aol.com.